WOULD YOU RATHER...?

The Sexy & Naughty Conversation Game for Couples

Hot & Flirty Edition

© 2020 by JL
All right reserved

This "Would you rather?" Questions created just for couples to get to know each other better.

If you're new to this game, it's really easy to get the hang of it – Would You Rather is choosing between two alternatives. That is, Would you rather do this or Would you rather do that.

Take turns asking and answering the questions. You can choose only one of the options to answer, cannot skip or select both.

It's a great way of starting conversations and discovering preferences of your partner. You may be surprised to know the hidden side of your partner.

It's fun to play this game with a group of friends too. Let's see what answer you will get from them.

Would you rather...

be in a committed
relationship

or

be friends with
benefits?

Would you rather...

sleep with someone
twice your age

or

minor?

Would you rather...

sleep with alien

or

die a virgin?

Would you rather...

have sex with a corpse

or

never have sex again?

Would you rather...

live in a city

or

in the countryside?

Would you rather...

be with someone who is
overly optimistic

or

overly pessimistic?

Would you rather...

have multiple
average orgasms

or

have one absolutely
amazing orgasm?

Would you rather...

date someone
who's highly ambitious
about their career

or

someone who cares
more about passions
outside of work?

Would you rather...

make out
on a couch

or

make out
against the wall?

Would you rather...

have many kids

or

just one kid?

Would you rather...

kiss in public

or

kiss in private?

Would you rather...

go to swingers club

or

go to strip bar
with your partner?

Would you rather...

dance with your partner
with slow music

or

go wild with
retro disco music?

Would you rather...

read poetry with your
partner at home

or

go sailing together
on the lake?

Would you rather...

have your partner
massage your feet with oil

or

have a long hot bath
with him/her?

Would you rather...

be the last two people
in a zombie apocalypse

or

be on a stranded island?

Would you rather...

be with a dumb
wealthy partner

or

a smart broke one?

Would you rather...

share a toothbrush
with your partner

or

have to wear
your partner's underwear?

Would you rather...

be told
where you are going
on a date

or

be surprised
on a date?

Would you rather...

date for a long time

or

get into a relationship
as soon as possible?

Would you rather...

have sex on the
airplane bathroom

or

have sex in a
moving car?

Would you rather...

know every secret
your partner has

or

are some secrets
better left uncovered?

Would you rather...

get your
dream job

or

dream partner?

Would you rather...

date someone who has
the same religious
orientation as you

or

would you
not mind at all?

Would you rather...

get your
dream job

or

dream partner?

Would you rather...

date someone who has
the same religious
orientation as you

or

would you
not mind at all?

Would you rather...

skip work for
a romantic date

or

date for office work?

Would you rather...

be with someone
funny

or

attractive?

Would you rather...

be with a loud partner

or

an overly shy partner?

Would you rather...

have 2 minutes of foreplay
and 20 minutes of sex

or

have 20 minutes of forplay
and 2 minutes of sex?

Would you rather...

have lots of children

or

lots of pets?

Would you rather...

cut all ties with your ex

or

be friends with them?

Would you rather...

have sex without love

or

love without sex?

Would you rather...

be rich and ugly

or

poor and good-looking?

Would you rather...

have sex with someone
who is super good looking
but unskilled in bed

or

have sex with someone
who is super skilled in bed
but very ugly?

Would you rather...

have sex from
the front only

or

from behind only?

Would you rather...

your partner cook
breakfast in bed for you

or

prepare romantice
dinner for you?

Would you rather...

be with someone who
overly sensitive

or

overly insensitive?

Would you rather...

have sex under shower

or

sex in a bathtub?

Would you rather...

be in an unbalanced
relationship where you love
your partner more

or

he/she loves you more?

Would you rather...

be with a
jealous partner

or

a distant one?

Would you rather...

be with an
ambitious partner

or

a funny one?

Would you rather...

be a night owl

or

an early riser?

Would you rather...

your partner
buy you a gift

or

make you one?

Would you rather...

have sex in
a jacuzzi bathtub
outside the house

or

in a kitchen?

Would you rather...

be with someone
who snores loudly

or

has bad breath?

Would you rather...

be with a partner
who never shaves

or

one who never cuts
their toenails?

Would you rather...

be with a partner who
have a tattoo of his/her ex

or

have to tell your parents
you met on Tinder?

Would you rather...

be with a partner who is
stupid but in shape

or

overweight with
einstein's brain?

Would you rather...

have a partner who
hates pets

or

loves them more than you?

Would you rather...

faint during an
important presentation
to your managers

or

at your wedding?

Would you rather...

have a romantic and sexy
candlelit dinner with
your partner

or

participate in
a heart pounding activity
like sky-diving with
your partner?

Would you rather...

have a lifetime
subscription to Netflix

or

free Starbucks daily?

Would you rather...

try something new and exciting in the bedroom

or

have a new hobby with your partner?

Would you rather...

go on more
romantic dates

or

go on more
fun dates?

Would you rather...

have to eat pizza
for one meal every day

or

never again?

Would you rather...

have sex with
light on

or

all the light off?

Would you rather...

orgasm with
oral sex

or

give an orgasm
through oral sex?

Would you rather...

have quick
early morning sex

or

long late night sex?

Would you rather...

get caught having sex
in public

Or

find out that you
were being watched
after the fact?

Would you rather...

have sex with partner
who is noisy
throughout sex

or

partner who only
screams during
an orgasm?

Would you rather...

your parents hated
your partner

or

your partner hated
your parents?

Would you rather...

have a partner
who is a great cook and
messy around the house

or

a horrible cook but neat?

Would you rather...

have perpetual orgasm
that never-ending

or

never have another orgasm
for the rest of your life?

Would you rather...

have a sex phone
with your partner

Or

a one-night stand
with stranger?

Would you rather...

have a conservative
sex life

or

add more fun to
your sex life with
sex toys?

Would you rather...

have ice-cream eaten
off your body

or

eat it off your
partner's body?

Would you rather...

have sex with
long sensation foreplay

or

have rough and
hardcore sex?

Would you rather...

kiss on the first date

or

wait a few dates?

Would you rather...

cuddle under the moon

or

make out under the moon?

Would you rather...

travel around the world

or

have a family?

Would you rather...

sleep under the stars

or

stay in a hotel?

Would you rather...

meet the love of your life
in high school

or

at 30?

Would you rather...

make your partner
jealous of someone

or

make everyone else
jealous of your partner?

Would you rather...

lay in bed waiting
for your partner
in something sexy

or

stark naked?

Would you rather...

receive a piece of jewelry

or

a room makeover
for an anniversary?

Would you rather...

spend a holiday
alone with your partner
or

with family?

Would you rather...

have separate hobbies

or

one together?

Would you rather...

go to your high school
reunion alone

or

with your partner?

Would you rather...

tell your lover a white lie
to spare feelings

or

blurt out the truth?

Would you rather...

write your own
wedding vows

or

copy from a website?

Would you rather...

forgive your partner

or

harbor a grudge
if you found out that
he/she lies to you?

Would you rather...

your partner
be abducted by aliens

or

held for ransom
by the mob?

Would you rather...

your partner sound like
parakeet when laughing

or

coughs like a bull
when snorting?

Would you rather...

come home to dinner
on the table

or

ushered out to your
favorite restaurant?

Would you rather...

find your partner waiting
in a bubble bath

or

all packed for a surprise
weekend getaway?

Would you rather...

spend the day
with your partner
being pampered at a spa

or

enjoying a workout
at the gym?

Would you rather...

spend the evening
with your partner
playing a video game

or

cuddle together
reading a book?

Would you rather...

be with a partner who
likes to dress comfortably

or

a partner who likes
to dress fashionably?

Would you rather...

date someone
with no emotions

or

date a compulsive liar?

Would you rather...

be in a bad relationship
for the rest of your life

or

have no relationship
for the rest of your life?

Would you rather...

fall in love with someone
who's allergic to all
of your favorite food

or

allergic to pets?

Would you rather...

follow your heart

or

your head while making important decisions about your love life?

Would you rather...

experience
unrequited love

or

never know how
it feels to be in love?

Would you rather...

keep searching for
true love and keep
getting heartbroken

or

give up searching
after the first heartbreak?

Would you rather...

tell your partner
the bitter truth

or

comfort him/her with lies?

Would you rather...

marry a doctor

or

an athlete?

Would you rather...

be with someone who's confrontational and places the problem right on the table

or

someone who approaches issues between you in a more careful, gentle way?

Would you rather...

date a good kisser

or

date a good lover?

Would you rather...

give a strip tease

or

get a strip tease?

Would you rather...

say "I love you"
to your partner

or

show your partner just
how much
you love him/her?

Would you rather...

be handcuffed to the bed
by your partner

or

handcuff your partner
to the bed?

Would you rather...

make out in a hotel's pool

or

in a hotel room's balcony?

Would you rather...

make your partner moan

or

make your partner laugh?

Would you rather...

be in a serious relationship
with a playboy/playgirl

or

be in an open relationship
with a playboy/playgirl?

Would you rather...

get compliments from
a lot of people at a club

or

get compliments from
just your crush?

Would you rather...

be the most sought after

or

have the most sought-after
person as a partner?

www.ingramcontent.com/pod-product-compliance
Lightning Source LLC
Chambersburg PA
CBHW052110150726
48002CB00006B/2292